The Art of Mindful Eating

How to transform your relationship with food and
start eating mindfully

Cinzia Pezzolesi & Ivana Placko

ISBN-13: 978-1511538855

ISBN-10: 1511538856

Table of Contents

Foreword

Eating is a core part of our life and for some people this activity is undertaken without thought. For some it is an act that causes immense suffering and can be depleting rather than nourishing. For some, the impulse to eat, to nourish the body, is something to be dominated and controlled. Mindful eating, on the other hand, is about working with, instead of against, our body and our need to eat.

The Art of Mindful Eating does not tell you what you can and can't eat, but invites you to develop awareness of your choices around food. By eating mindfully we become more in tune with our bodies and therefore more in harmony with life.

I love the authors' non-judgmental approach to what 'right' and what's 'wrong' and taking the readers through the journey of self-discovery. I feel compassionate towards many people who struggle with food, but only look for outside sources of wisdom, instead of looking for their natural wisdom. Unlike typical diet books that have a standard prescription and a set of recipes, it's refreshing to hear that there is no one size fits all approach to developing a positive relationship with food and it's about taking into account individuals behind them. By the end of the book, every reader will come out with something different which is inspiring and emphasis the uniqueness of our eating experiences.

Thank you Cinzia and Ivana, I am a big fan and I am looking forward to incorporating some of your techniques into my daily routine.

Raymond Aaron

NY Times Bestselling Author

Chapter 1: Introduction to Mindful Eating

"Start where you are. Use what you have. Do what you can." - A. Ashe

Eating is complex. Overeating is even more complex. Both can be challenging. We have learned to solve the challenge of eating using food to provide our body with energy. And we have learned to solve the problem of overeating through dieting. This book is about questioning the solutions we have applied so far that have become problematic in their own right, and about developing the art of mindful eating. After all, dieting is an art, not a science. Sure, there is a lot of science behind the art, but it is an art nonetheless. With so many food combinations and other external variables such as our genetics, age, gender and physical activity levels, there can be virtually no scientific prescription for a perfect diet that will work for everyone.

The intent of this book is to help you find out what works for you and how you can make small lifestyle changes that will help you develop a joyful and relaxed relationship with food, without the struggle.

This work was inspired by the experiences of professional athletes and young women. This is our story, in brief.

Cinzia

I am a clinical psychologist, but I was a professional volleyball player for over 15 years. Being a volleyball player meant that a great part of my life gravitated around trainings and games for several hours a day and that the rest of my time was spent studying or thinking and planning my next meal.

As I child, I was told that I was 'really beautiful' and my parents were proud of showing me to their friends. Growing up, I noticed that many other people would compliment me on the way I looked, and that my appearance would guarantee me invitations to the most glamorous parties to hang out with the hippest crowd and get me memberships to exclusive clubs. Admittedly, it did not take long to build my identity around that 'perfect body' that was so efficient when it came to performing in a volleyball court and so helpful in my social interactions.

Eating and food were so important to me – perhaps more than important. Food was, for me, the biggest reward, a source of comfort, punishment and happiness all in one. It had the power to determine my body shape and, consequently, my social life and achievements in sport. A meal could make me feel great or miserable and, more often than not, both feelings would coexist.

I also remember periods of time in which I would see certain types of food as dangerous, and something to stay well away from. I was not allowed to have the chocolate bars or other sweets that I naturally loved. 'Chocolate is an aliment to be consumed with parsimony, once every two weeks as a maximum' my coach would say. I could ruminate on those warning words for days, especially when the team's personal trainer would check on my weight and record it on a very noticeable whiteboard in my gym every Monday.

I would never buy the food I really wanted for fear of overeating, perhaps ignoring the requests of my body. It gave me the unpleasant feeling of being powerless in front of that ice cream tub or packet of biscuits. The script was often the same, once I started to eat them, I would go all the way and have the whole tub of ice cream or packet of biscuits as I had already blown my 'try to keep fit' efforts for that day. This was often followed by guilt and shame that would last until the day after or even for the rest of that week.

Ivana

My obsession with food started when, as a perfectly healthy teenage athlete, I discovered magazines and books that talked about potentially increasing your performance by changing your diet. Back then, in the 90s, whole grains and complex carbs where the 'good guys' and fat in all forms was considered 'bad'. That was before Mr Google, so it was the only information I could get my hands on. As a perfectionist who wanted to do everything that was in my control to improve my performance, I followed everything I read to a T.

Moving to America to play volleyball at a college level perpetuated my growing obsession with food. By American volleyball standards, I was considered to be too thin, and I loved that categorisation. I took the infamous 'Freshman 15' to a new level and, despite 3+ hours of daily intense volleyball trainings, I managed to gain almost 30lbs during my freshman year. A buffet style cafeteria with unlimited food options, including ice cream and chocolate I would normally get only on special occasions in Croatia, became daily treats. In addition, there were so many food options and flavours I had never heard of before, so I just wanted to try everything. My thought was - I deserved it. After all, I trained so hard and spent all day studying, so food was often used as a reward. I also used food as an escape - I missed my family and friends back in Croatia and food was just so comforting that it helped me forget how much. Food portions in restaurants and supermarkets did not help and I often let that dictate how much I ate, instead of listening to what my body needed.

Food became my go-to escape for an immediate reward or temporary relief for any sort of discomfort. Going back to Croatia and hearing comments about my 'healthy' weight wasn't easy. I became really self-conscious about my weight and obsessed with eating healthily, so I went through cycles of restricting 'unhealthy' foods in my diet, which ended up in unhealthy binges followed by a lot of guilt.

Looking back, we can see that we were just trying the best we could to feel comfortable in our own skins and to fit in in our environment. After many years of misadventures and having tried pretty much every possible diet or fashionable cleansing programme, we came to regard dieting as an art form and a way for us to express ourselves. Now, we have decided to spread the word on how we eventually made friends with food and started on the amazing path of mindful eating.

The mindful eating path

The origins and the evidence base

When talking about mindful eating, it is almost impossible not to mention the links with mindfulness as core element of the path towards a balanced and joyful relationship with food. Mindfulness is 'pure awareness', and it has been defined as 'a way of paying attention in the present moment, intentionally and non-judgmentally' (Kabat-Zinn, 1999).Mindfulness has its origins in the Buddhist tradition but its practice is not religious or esoteric in nature.

Mindfulness is indeed an inherent human capacity, and its goal is to maintain moment-to-moment awareness in the everyday experience. Various techniques, classified as formal and informal practices, can be used to focus the mind. Formal practice draws from disciplines such as meditation, yoga and qigong, an ancient Chinese healing art involving controlled breathing and slow movement exercises. Informal practice requires paying sustained attention to activities in one's daily routine, for example, when walking to the train station in the morning, one may try to be aware of all the sensations in the present moment such as the fresh air, the noise of one's footsteps or of the surrounding people. This ability to maintain awareness throughout our lives allows us to develop an 'approach' orientation towards our experience, to develop the habit of bringing a warm, kindly curiosity to whatever occurs in the mind, body and the world around us. This leads us to reach greater overall levels of health and happiness, and these positive effects of mindfulness on health and wellbeing have been comprehensively demonstrated in literature (Mental Health Foundation, 2010; Davidson RJ et al. 2003; Hölzela BK et al. 2011; Nataraja S. 2008).

Mindful eating is about developing a very personal relationship with food that is based on curiosity, kindness and self-compassion. It is about 'allowing yourself to become aware of the positive and nurturing opportunities that are available through food selection and preparation by respecting your own inner wisdom' (TCME, 2014).

Recent studies have shown that mindful eating can improve or extend long term health outcomes in people with eating disorders (Godsey, 2013). For example, over 20 years, Professor Kristeller and her research group (2006; 2011; 2012) found that their mindful eating programme reduced the lack of physiological self-awareness of satiety and the use of food for nonnutritive reasons that sustain the binge eating cycle. They also found that mindful eating increases the ability to disengage automatic and often dysfunctional reactivity that would lead to overeating or restricting, thus allowing the development of wiser and more balanced relationships with ourselves, our eating and our bodies.

Listening to our wise body and to the innate, almost intuitive knowledge of what we really need to create our wellbeing is often something that we ignore or simply forget to do. As we are attempting to squeeze in a 10 minutes lunch break in our busy schedules or eat a snack whilst typing an email, we miss out on opportunities to connect to that innate knowledge.

The mindful eating approach could be helpful to overcome the tendency of eating while multitasking and comfort eating, both of which are mindless rather than mindful.

It might now be tempting to think that eating mindfully is the only way to eat healthily and that this could never be achieved through eating. But looking into the complex mechanics of human function, into the multitasking miracle of human life, we can see how mindlessness makes sense too. To spare our minds the constant trouble of deciding on a myriad of choices, to conserve energy and to optimise performance, we automate ourselves. Having to make approximately 200 choices a day regarding food, eating is one aspect of our functioning that we have automated. The problem with automated and, thus, mindless eating, however, is that conserving energy in today's sedentary world leads to a range of health issues. So as we focus on mindful eating, let us wave a fond farewell to mindless eating. After all, it is this mindless eating that helped us through many business lunches where fully automated eating algorithms allowed us to skillfully handle pasta with red sauce while rattling off bulleted versions of our work lives. It is this mindless eating that allowed us to have many dinner dates where we eloquently navigated through the courses of our relationship history without noticing a wine stain on our evening wear. It is this mindless eating that has allowed our blindfolded fingertips to find the last cashew in a jar of mixed nuts without pausing our favorite movie scene. At the same time, it is probably mindless eating that made that snack disappear, leaving no trace apart from a colourful plastic bag, and leaving us somewhat dissatisfied.

Through the practice of mindful eating, you could develop a new, more adaptive habit of eating with the full intention of getting to the point where the decision to be mindful about eating is evoked automatically and effortlessly. It is important, however, to underline that, like any habit, mindful eating is a learning curve, and it requires patience and an open mind through each step of the change process.

The relationship between mindful eating and diets

One thing we have learnt the hard way is that traditional diets do not work. If they did, the industry would probably not proliferate as it does, but would eventually go out of business. Diets only work for a short period of time until we can handle the frustration of eating in a prescribed way. Moreover, the prescribed way is often dictated by the trend of the moment. Sometimes it's fat that gets put under the spotlight, so we might walk down any aisle in our local supermarket and see plenty of fat-free desserts or low-fat biscuits that are meant to help us with watching our weight, managing our cholesterol levels or eating for a healthy heart. We might, however, end up eating sugar-loaded biscuits and high glycemic index ready meals that would send our blood sugar levels through the roof, leaving us feeling tired or at risk of developing health problems, including type 2 diabetes, obesity and high blood pressure. Perhaps we could turn to high-protein diets that could affect our liver and kidneys. Sometimes we hear that the body needs a rest and that fasting could be beneficial, but we also hear about the importance of having regular meals. The list is of do's and don'ts is endless, and what seems to be apparent is that there is not a 'right' diet for everyone; and most importantly, there is a need for a completely new paradigm that goes beyond the 'what' to eat and also explores with curiosity and kindness the 'why' we eat to help us reconnect with our bodies as harmonious vehicles of our souls.

The mindful eating approach is an awareness-building and gentle habit-modifying process aimed at improving our relationship with food. It could be helpful to overcome overeating, under-eating or other unhelpful eating behaviours. Mindful eating is not a diet, at least, not in the modern sense of the word. The approach can be, however, used as a diet facilitator. Before we explain

THE ART OF MINDFUL EATING

what we mean by the term 'diet facilitator', let us clarify what was originally meant by the word 'diet'.

Dieta, in Latin, means 'a way of living'. Therefore, in its original meaning, a diet presupposes a permanent change in the way (or style) of life that preserves a way (or style) of life worth living. Geneen Roth, an anti-dieting pioneer, suggests that for a diet to work, it cannot feel like a diet. While mindful eating can facilitate diet compliance, it is, at its basis, a dieta; a lifestyle or a way of living. By definition, it does not negatively interfere with quality of life; instead it promotes sustainable changes in our eating patterns that will lead to a healthier and happier lifestyle.

Most modern weight-management systems, known as 'diets' are not quite diets in this sense. These diets can be subdivided into two distinct components or phases: an induction phase and a maintenance phase. The induction phase usually involves some kind of restriction of foods and/or portion sizes. If endured, the induction phase results in a relatively rapid weight loss. The maintenance phase is a recommended way of living that allows the dieter to maintain the target weight following the induction-phase weight reduction. With this distinction in mind, it could be said that the induction phase is not really a diet in the original sense of the word. Indeed, it would be hard to imagine anyone realistically maintaining a crash-diet regimen indefinitely and still call it 'living'. The maintenance phase, with its long-term focus and with its more realistic approach to food is closer to the original meaning of the word diet'. The maintenance phase is not, however, what a typical person has in mind when he or she goes on a diet.

Most people view dieting as the only solution, a time-limited sprint towards weight loss rather than a lifelong journey towards health. As we go on a diet, we might think tactically, not strategically: we are thinking not of a lifelong commitment to a particular way of living but, rather, of mobilising just enough motivation and self-discipline to endure a sprint so that we can fit into a reference-point piece of clothing, such as a pair of jeans worn in high school, a wedding dress or that spring-break bikini from college. The mindful eating concept it is an approach to living that can be useful in facilitating both the induction and the maintenance phases of your weight-management.

The art of eating mindfully

In the attempt to summarise a complex and fascinating topic such as food and eating behaviours, we are suggesting here our very personal selection of 'mindful eating essentials' that can be used as a guide, invitation or just as reflection points during your path of self-discovery. These are:

- Explore your eating patterns with compassion and curiosity
- Eat with all your senses
- Reconnect with your physical hunger and satiety cues
- Make mindful choices around food
- Eat and live with awareness

We will describe each of the mindful eating essentials in the chapters that follow, and whether these principles sound simple or confusing right now, we are inviting you to remain open and curious throughout this book. The book will conclude with a chapter on how to take these 'essentials' forward and how to overcome potential barriers to eat mindfully.

NOTE

Should You Be Using This Book If You Are on a Diet?

You've probably experienced the cycle before. You've been off the diet for a few weeks and now you're being bad. Now you don't have to worry about counting calories, you're treating yourself to naughty foods and reclaiming your social life and your freedom. But as your 'freedom high' wears off, you begin to experience increasing feelings of guilt

---

that rain all over your post-diet parade.

One of the main reasons diets tend not to work is because they don't take into account the people behind them. They don't care about our stories or our personalities – they just impose themselves on us with no consideration for our individuality. Diets force us to change our lives quickly, without any gradual steps, and this often leads to failure. We are given no time to practise, but simply thrown in at the deep end and left to either sink or swim. More often than not, we sink.

So if you are on a diet, or planning on dieting in the future, make this time different by considering the mindful eating approach. Unlike typical diets, mindful eating is like an art form, understanding that before it can be mastered, it must be practised. Mindful eating allows you the time to do this – teaching you how to change your diet and your attitude so that you may lead a healthier, happier life. It is likely that you have probably experienced the cycle. Off another diet for a few weeks, you have been "bad." Whether or not you lost weight while on the diet, you are probably looking forward to the regained quality of life and freedom to eat whatever and whenever. But the high of this freedom has been wearing off a sense of guilt starts to slowly take away the idyllic picture.

Chapter 2: Explore Your Eating Patterns with Compassion and Curiosity

"Out beyond ideas of wrongdoing and rightdoing, there is a field. I'll meet you there." - Rumi

Why do we eat?

Asking "Why do we eat?" rather than "How much should we eat?" or "What should we eat?" could be a good starting point for anyone who is interested in developing a good relationship with food. We might say: "I eat because I get hungry, and to provide my body with energy." Yes, the main biological idea behind eating is to pump fuel into our bodies so it can perform the functions of life. That is a great theory, but in practice, however, our reasons for eating often have often very little to do with the needs of our body. There are in fact several reasons why we eat.

We Eat to Satisfy the Needs of the Body

As mentioned, we are really perfect machines, programmed to eat out of physiological hunger: a straightforward, undeniable need for energy that results in physiologically triggered eating, the sole purpose of which is to satisfy the needs of the body.

We also experience hunger in different ways, but research tends to show that it's very easy to get 'tricked' into eating food even if you're not physically hungry, such as when you see a favourite food or notice that it's time to eat.

We Eat to Satisfy the Needs of the Mind

We eat out of psychological hunger. Our minds need to be entertained, comforted or distracted, resulting in psychologically triggered eating, the sole purpose of which is to satisfy the needs of the mind, even if the needs of the mind are satisfied at a cost to the body.

We Eat out of Habit

A habit can be understood as a stimulus-response relationship in which a stimulus is an element of the environment that triggers us to respond in a previously conditioned, mindless manner. For example, since cinemas traditionally sell popcorn and soda, we associate going to the movies (stimulus) with eating popcorn and drinking soda (response). When we eat out of habit in response to an external trigger, our eating is initiated by the demand of the environment. The environment demands that we eat now and we automatically respond. When we let the environment decide when we should eat, we are, in a sense, reducing the range of our conscious choices to eventually find out that, very often, we were not even hungry.

Why do we overeat?

"I keep wanting more and more. It's as if I'm walking toward this invisible line that says, "Enough." I keep eating and eating to get there. Then, I turn around and

realise I'm so far past the line that I can't even see it." –
Jordan

There are differences in our appetite levels, our
metabolisms and lifestyles. If we put these differences
aside for a moment, on a behavioural level, overeating is
often triggered by the environment, intense emotions,
stress and difficulties in tuning in with our body feedback
to help self-regulating, for example, a lack of awareness
of the sensations of hunger and fullness.

Let's look at some of these triggers and how these affect
your lifestyle. We are inviting you to be explorative and
curious about your patterns rather than judgmental.

Environmental Triggers

Imagine a friend invites you out to eat. You aren't actually
hungry, but decide to go along. Once at the restaurant,
the sights and smells provoke an intense appetite. "I am
famished!" you might say, unaware of the hidden
evolution of a want into a need. The dinner is over and
you feel full, but your friend isn't finished. She wants to

look at the dessert menu. Minutes later, seduced by the pictures of beautiful desserts, the new question is what to choose amongst those wonderful cakes rather than whether you want to have a dessert at all. What happened? You saw something appetising and developed a desire for it, or a craving, that was strong enough to convince you it was hunger. Sound familiar? The point is that the environment (a combination of people, places and foods) can encourage us to eat when we are not hungry (initial overeating) and maintain our eating past the point of fullness (continued overeating). Perhaps it is worth spending a moment to explain the difference between hunger-driven and craving-driven eating. Craving-driven eating may be conscious or unconscious. You might see food and eat it just because it's there, without even realising it, which would be a case of mindless grazing. Or you might see the food, experience a craving, recognise that you are not hungry, and make a conscious choice to eat anyway. In contrast, hunger-driven eating is always conscious: hunger, as a physiological imperative, commands the presence of the mind.

What are your environmental eating triggers?

External eating triggers, or the environmental stimuli that pull the strings of our appetite and provoke cravings, can be divided into the following categories: food characteristics, activities, settings (places), events, time and weather. What are your personal eating triggers?

Food characteristics that trigger eating

Some food characteristics, such as smell and taste, naturally trigger our appetite. Others, such as the look of food, may have an acquired craving-inducing power. Take M&M's, for example., With their waxy, artificial colouring, they seem more like toys than food. Clearly, you first have to learn that these little multi-coloured marbles are food before you can actually crave them. As an experiment, you could explore the trigger value of certain food characteristics and discover the sensory modalities that tend to activate your cravings.

Activities that trigger eating

Many activities can trigger eating. The discussion below may help you identify the type of activities that trigger your appetite.

TV viewing

Watching TV while snacking is an entertainment formula that has spoilt many a diet. If, one day, TV manufacturers discover a way to make television emit smell, our stomachs will probably start to resemble the boxy TVs of yesteryear.

Reading

Eating has come to augment our leisurely reading and console us when we have to read as a chore, such as when studying or reading for work. Reading and eating has also enjoyed a cultural stamp of approval: a newspaper for breakfast symbolises an idyllic morning. Even coffee houses, historically marketed as conversation forums, have become reading rooms where coffee no longer stimulates conversation, but only accompanies us and our laptops.

Entertainment

Traveling circuses, gladiator fights and theatrical performances of the past may have made way for today's sporting events such as rodeos, dog/horse/car races, and movie-going, but the combination of the visual and the gustatory remains the same. While the times have changed the menus, the marriage of entertainment and food appears to be everlasting.

Socialising

Family dinners, dinners out with friends, business lunches, diplomatic receptions, neighbourhood barbecues and romantic picnics are some of the classic forms of social eating. Sure, eating is a good way to bond; after all, hunger is a common denominator, but perhaps it is also worth considering and cultivating non-eating common denominators in our relationships.

Are you a social eater? Do you tend to eat when others eat? Do you primarily socialise through eating out? Do you try to please people by agreeing to their invitations to eat when you are not actually hungry? Do you tend to overeat when you're with company? Monitor your social-eating habits for a couple of weeks to gauge the impact of company on your appetite. If you feel you are easily susceptible to indulge as a result of peer pressure, rehearse some assertive yet tactful limit setting. One more tip: if overeating during work lunches has been a particular issue for you, try eating lunch alone and, to maintain your friendships outside of the workplace, offer to go for a walk with your former lunch partners instead.

Thinking and problem solving

When you have something on your mind, it's not unusual to end up with something in your mouth. Problem solving, as a work-related activity, often leads to eating. Somebody calls for a brainstorming session, and before you know it, the think tank becomes the eat tank. Do we think better when we eat? Or do we just balance out the chore of thinking with the comfort of eating? Think about and monitor this under-recognised trigger of overeating in the weeks to come.

Places that trigger eating

Have you noticed how eating in the kitchen can differ from eating in the living room, how eating-in differs from eating-out and how eating-out at a backyard barbecue differs from eating out at a company picnic? Not only is our eating triggered by certain places, but also certain places trigger different rules of eating engagement, as well as the amounts we are socially expected to eat.

Eating establishments are professionally designed to stimulate your appetite, whether you are hungry or not.

Restaurants, cafes, bistros, bars and diners have the greatest convergence of eating triggers. Your own eating establishment may be anywhere in your home, a certain recliner, the kitchen, your bedroom or your work desk. What place have you turned into an eating establishment by associating it with eating? Consider this and be open to any ideas that might emerge.

Times of day that trigger eating

Times of day also trigger our eating. We eat not by our body clocks, but by the actual clock. We eat in the morning, not because we are hungry, but because we are supposed to have breakfast in the morning. We lunch around noon, not because we necessarily need food at that time, but because it is lunchtime, and lunchtime, by definition, is for eating lunch. We arrange our suppers around family members' schedules or TV shows. Times of day not only trigger us to eat but also influence how much we eat. Imagine filling up your car with petrol because you consulted the clock instead of your petrol gauge. You would simply decide it was time to pull into the petrol station and fill up the car, regardless of whether the car has gone anywhere or stayed in the garage. Of course, this approach would not work with cars, given their limited tanks, but our stomachs can stretch several times their size and accommodate a vast amount of food we do not really need.

You could try this: for a couple of weeks, keep track of when you eat and whether this, in fact, coincides with when you feel hungry. Also, consider experimenting, if only for a couple of weeks, with shifting from a time-based decision to eat ("it's time to eat") to a physiologically more intuitive idea ("I am hungry enough to eat now").

Weather as an eating trigger

There is something appetite-provoking about inclement weather. Have you noticed a pattern of craving comfort food when it rains or snows or storms outside? Perhaps it's about a sense of control: by making ourselves comfortable inside, we defy the harshness of nature, persuading ourselves that we can survive it and that we can stay in control of life, despite nature's unpredictability. Explore whether weather influences your appetite and how.

***

Mindful activity

Try this activity for the following 2 weeks:

Follow the tracks of your eating to find your environmental triggers. For the next two weeks, after you eat, ask yourself why you ate. After two weeks, make a note of any patterns you noticed or jot down what you have learnt about your key trigger vulnerabilities. To remember your insights, think of a way to label your craving pattern. Are you a "TV-watching eater," an "eater-outer," or a "by-the-clock eater?" To help you better identify which trigger activated your behaviour, refer to the summary of triggers below:

- Food characteristics: smells, sights, sounds

- Activities: TV, reading, thinking, problem-solving, socialising
- Settings: indoors (eating in, eating out), outdoors (barbecue, picnic, drive-through)
- Events: holidays, birthdays, weddings, parties, , stress days, days off
- Time: breakfast time, brunch time, lunchtime, dinnertime, suppertime, night time
- Weather: inclement weather, picnic weather

***

Emotional triggers

Here's a thought: eating to relieve stress works! If the strategy of eating to cope didn't work, we would not have a problem with misusing it. What doesn't work, however, is overeating when we are stressed.

Emotional eating can be defined as "eating for reasons other than hunger". Sure, it would be optimal not to use food to cope with other emotions and life events, but in the meantime, as you work on this long-term goal of a

CINZIA PEZZOLESI, IVANA PLACKO

flexible coping style, approach your habit of emotional eating with compassion. Before you try to give up emotional eating, we could try to make better use of this coping strategy by becoming a more mindful, emotional eater. Emotional eating isn't a problem, but mindless emotional eating might be!

It is indeed normal amongst the general population to eat, or drink to reflect our emotions, for example to celebrate an achievement or a birthday, to share important moments of our lives or to handle a bad day. Balanced eaters are also emotional eaters, but research has demonstrated that they tend to compensate for their emotional eating at a later stage, perhaps having lighter meals because they are not as hungry as usual or by increasing their physical activity during the week. Also, it is noticeable that people who do not struggle with food use several other copying mechanisms to handle stress and emotions.

As Cathy, one of our participants said: "As a little kid, whenever I had a bad day, my mother and I would sit down at the kitchen table and eat chocolate wafers together. This pattern followed me into adulthood. When I had a bad day at work or a disagreement with my boyfriend, my mind would automatically say I needed chocolate! I turned this around by using another method of soothing myself. At first, nothing felt as good as eating. But then I slowly realised that chocolate cookies are not the only pick-me-up available."

For many of us, comfort eating is our Achilles' heel. A bit of stress hits, or a sense of being lonely, and we reach for something sugary, fatty or salty. Some foods specifically trigger the reward and pleasure areas of the brain.

But what are we actually looking for?

Like Cathy, we are all looking for some type of comfort. We seek comfort in so many ways, sometimes in healthier ways, like calling a friend, but often in less helpful ways, like numbing ourselves with the help of drugs, alcohol, food, the Internet and so on. Easing pain and discomfort with food has become very common. Some of the main treatments for drug or alcohol addiction name abstinence as the main therapeutic goal but, unfortunately, we cannot abstain from food, hence it is important to befriend it.

Eating comfort foods in small portions is generally not a problem. Macaroni and cheese and hot brownies are fun and taste good, but turning to comfort food as your primary source of stress relief becomes an issue that can lead to ill health and distress. There is in fact, a very fine line between having a very pleasurable meal and turning it into an uncomfortable and depleting experience.

How to handle emotional eating

As illustrated above, most people use emotional eating as an attempt at emotional self-regulation, motivated by a desire to change how they feel. One alternative way of addressing the presence of intense emotions and returning to a more manageable baseline, is to maintain moment–to-moment awareness of the 'here and now'.. Our natural tendency to worry about the future or to catastrophise often takes us away from the events that have created the strong emotions or stress, and triggers a cascade of reactions that makes the situation even more stressful.

"I've tried begging, pleading and bribing myself not to snack. If I promise myself one bite, it turns into five more. When I'm totally desperate and frustrated with myself, I blow up. I yell at myself. I rant and rave, and start threatening myself with severe punishments to try to deter myself from eating: no dinner, or sometimes, no shopping for a month." - Melanie

Or you might have experienced the following scenario: you are at a party, where you do not know many people, or your friends are late and you spend a long period of time standing alone with your drink. It feels uncomfortable and awkward to be there alone. You notice there is a wonderful buffet and decide to help yourself as you wait for your friends. You indulge in a few more canapés than you were planning on eating to ease these uncomfortable feelings. You begin to feel guilty, thinking that you should not have started your evening in this way, and you feel like a failure for slipping off your diet. These intense sensations can go on for several hours until your party is ruined. Once you are back at home, you open the fridge and finish the leftovers from the day before, feeling out of control.

Bringing awareness to the different aspects of our experience will help your handle the situation in a more skilful way and lead you to copying strategies and behaviours to stop the situation becoming worse. We can see this graphically illustrated in the diagram below:

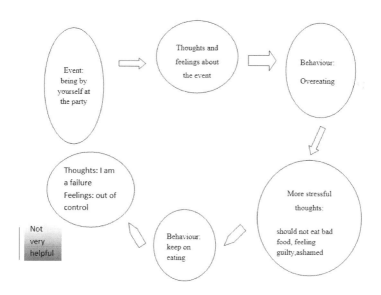

The practice below, that in formal mindfulness practices would usually be called a 'three-step breathing space", can be helpful in bringing awareness to our mental processes and create space for considered actions rather than going down the usual routes. We are adding a self-caring element by inviting you to bring awareness to your actual needs that, once fulfilled, will make you feel nourished rather than depleted. The 'three-step breathing space for self-care' is a short practice that can last between two minutes and ten minutes.

***

Three-step breathing space for self-care

Sit in a comfortable position, with your feet flat on the floor, and with your eyes closed, if you prefer. Begin to notice your breathing and the flow of air that enters your nose and gently travels all the way down to your lungs. Breathe in this relaxed way for at least five breaths, sensing the fresh air coming in through your nose and letting go of any tension.

It could be helpful to have your hands on your belly or your chest to notice the gentle movements that accompany your breathing.

Now, checking-in with your mind and body, ask yourself: 'What is going on with me right now? What are my thoughts? Where do I feel them in my body?

'What are my emotions? Where do I feel them in the body?'

Then, pay attention to your breathing, noticing it moving in and out your body for one or two minutes (or allow more time if you feel like it). When your mind wanders away from your breathing, just bring it back to the psychical sensations of the breathing in your body, with kindness and without judging yourself.

For the next step, gently expand your awareness to the present moment, to the space of your body in the room, to the space of your body in your chair and open your eyes if they were closed.

After reconnecting with this enhanced awareness, it might feel appropriate to ask yourself 'what do I need right now that could help me go through this difficult time?'

Take your time to find your answers and then ask yourself 'How can I act with awareness and self-compassion?'

***

This practice can be followed by some considered and self-compassionate actions - actions taken in full awareness, taking advantage of the mental space that you have created by interrupting the rumination of thoughts, and with a kind attitude toward yourself. Also, identifying what you need to go through a difficult time might immediately become available to you, however sometimes it might take longer. You could try to develop your own list of 'considerate and self-compassionate actions' to be used in times of difficulty. Some examples of this include doing something pleasurable: an activity that you enjoy or something that would give you a sense of satisfaction or mastery, such as cleaning, exercising or doing some work. You could pay attention to your breathing or bodily sensations with the intention of remaining focused on what you were doing.

What if we are eating to push away our emotions and feel numb?

The goal of traditional emotional eating is often to return to the emotional baseline, from feeling distressed to feeling normal. However, we can also find ourselves overeating in order to become numb, to feel nothing instead of 'feeling normal'. This is often the case with 'binge eating', a form of overeating that is typically characterised by eating an objectively large amount of food and by an accompanying feeling of loss of control.

With this in mind, a mere runaway emotional eating episode is not actually a binge. It's just a lapse of mindfulness. For an overeating episode to be a true binge, you would have to more or less knowingly pursue the goal of an altered state of consciousness; you'd have to want to eat yourself into a state of oblivion.

Why is this important to understand?

Well, mindfulness is fundamentally incompatible with a state of oblivion. In other words, it would be hard to infuse a degree of mindfulness into a binge without defeating the binge's purpose.

What this means is that if you want to binge to the point of oblivion, all you can really do to make it more psychologically helpful is to give yourself conscious permission to do so, or to postpone the binge.

Let's suppose that you've had a truly difficult day. You are at your wit's end: you've tried every coping strategy you know and you still feel bad. Or, perhaps, you made a decision that you are going to binge - not just eat to cope in moderation, but to go all the way - until you feel really stuffed and numb to everything inside and outside of you.

Here you have a few choices: give yourself the conscious permission to go ahead and proceed with the binge so that you will minimise the post binge regret that might trigger unhealthy, compensatory behaviours and/or another binge. You can also try postponing the binge by a few minutes. While you wait, ask yourself whether you could be satisfied with an emotional eating episode (e.g. eating something even if you are not hungry) instead of a full binge. If you decide that an emotional eating episode will not cut it for you, then proceed with the binge. If, however, you conclude that an emotional eating episode might actually do it for you, then attempt to have a mindful emotional eating episode. Challenge yourself to eventually extend the delay from, say, five minutes to ten or fifteen minutes and, maybe, even to a half hour. The longer you postpone the binge, the more likely you are to settle for an otherwise innocuous emotional eating episode, which would be a healthier choice than a binge.

Focus on craving

Have you ever bought a box of chocolates for your friend's birthday two weeks in advance and been unable to wait to open it? You open it and make a significant visit to the box even before the birthday arrives. You have therefore experienced the famous 'I can't resist' thoughts - impulsive thoughts that you act on immediately as your mind keeps saying 'I want it, I can't wait!'

Independently from the reasons why the urge to eat has developed (environment, emotions, etc.) it could be helpful to be curious about such 'impulsive thoughts'. A series of classic studies by renowned psychologist Walter Mischel provides helpful tips for understanding impulsive thoughts. Though Mischel and his colleagues conducted these studies in the 1960s, they are still informative today. The researchers put preschool children in a room alone with a tempting treat: a marshmallow. Then, they told the kids that if they waited until the adult came back into the room, they could have two marshmallows instead of one. Some kids ate the marshmallow immediately after the adult left the room. Others waited patiently. Mischel wanted to know why some kids were able to wait and others couldn't.

He wondered whether some of the kids had a special, innate ability to delay gratification. Instead, Mischel found that some kids simply had better coping skills, which helped them to manage their desire to eat the marshmallow. Many of these kids used distraction. When researchers watched the tapes, they saw that the kids sang to themselves, counted things in the room, or played with objects, all to keep their minds off the marshmallow.

The second successful technique for helping kids wait was to teach them to think about the marshmallow in a new way. The researcher told the children to think of the object as a cotton ball or cloud instead of a marshmallow. Kids who previously had trouble waiting were much more able to wait when they employed this technique. It cooled down their initial reaction to the treat.

When dealing with cravings, yet again, we have several choices that will strengthen your mindful eating practice:

- Mindfully wait. Postpone unhealthy eating by waiting for five, ten or fifteen minutes as described in the previous paragraph. As you wait for the craving to dissipate, breathe slowly. Count each breath as you inhale.

- You can use some of these same strategies to overpower your urges. Like the kids in the study, try using distraction to keep your mind busy. Mindfully shift your attention to more affirming thoughts instead of automatic thoughts like "Just eat it" or "I want it now". Find something to keep your hands and thoughts busy and out of the kitchen.

- If you feel creative, you can also use a second strategy from the marshmallow studies: visual imagery. For example, imagine whipped cream to be glue or spackle. Visualise a cookie as a wooden Frisbee. Approaching this playfully, using this technique not to scare you away from treats or to instil negative thinking about food, but as a way to help you avoid reacting automatically to the immediate impulse to eat.

Try to be compassionate - you are doing the best you can

Have you ever tried to define perfection? Perfection is a state of flawlessness, so immaculate and error-free that it cannot be improved upon. It might seem beyond reach, but actually, it isn't. If perfection is a state that cannot be improved upon, then, as strange as it sounds, any moment is perfect in the sense that it has already happened, and is therefore too late to improve upon.

Even though this current moment, as imperfect as it can be, is beyond improvement, the next one still can be better. But before you reject this coming moment as not good enough, allow yourself to accept the imperfect perfection of this moment. In this very moment, you are doing the best you can. If you could already cope with life's stresses without involving food, of course, you would! And right now, you are working on it. Looking at your eating with patterns and compassion and setting aside your judgment will help you shift from mindless, craving-driven, environmentally triggered eating to eating that is guided by conscious choices. But until then, give yourself a pat on the back; you are doing the best you can.

Chapter 3: Eating with all Our Senses

"I have no philosophy. I have senses." - F. Pessoa

With little time to spare, we try to optimise each moment of leisure in order to amplify the total pleasure experience. We do not just want to have something good to eat, we also want a side of conversation. Or we want to eat whilst being entertained. Unfortunately, the brain does not process information in this way. In fact, we move from one task or activity to another very fast, in an attempt to accomplish as many things as possible in the shortest time. The more the stimuli we are exposed to, the smaller amount of attention we have to spare on every single one of them.

As we are exploring the path of mindful eating, we are trying to increase our sensorial experiences linked to our food and increase our focus when we eat. A delicious dessert is gone without enjoyment as our eyes are fixated on the TV, and a great TV moment is lost on us while we dip our fries in ketchup. In this chapter, we will explore how we can engage our senses when eating. This could help us develop curiosity towards our food, improve our savouring skills, and enjoy what we eat like a connoisseur would. We will focus on how to explore the flavour of food, and the role of sight in appreciating it. Each of these targets has a complexity of its own that warrants separate coverage. We will begin with the aspect of flavour.

Flavour

Flavour is not the same as taste. In fact, it is an overall impression of these three different elements: taste, smell and texture. Taste is communicated by four taste receptors on your tongue that detect sweetness, bitterness, sourness, saltiness and umami. Smell is communicated by olfactory sensors in your nasal passages and is thought to account for a significant portion of the overall experience of flavour. The texture, or feel, of food is also an important part of its flavour.

Chemesthesis is a phenomenon in which the food in the mouth, in addition to acting on the taste receptors, also acts upon the receptors of other senses, such as touch. Thus, the mouth conveys tactile information about the texture of the food, such as whether the food is solid, liquid, crumbly, creamy or crackly, and whether it is drying, cooling, evaporating, irritating, spicy or astringent in the way it feels. The sensory experience of food's flavour is a treasure trove of mindful opportunities.

Our first sensory impression of a food often comes from its packaging. This is called sensation transference, a situation in which we project our sensory experience of the product's packaging onto the product itself. In a classic example, Louis Cheskin, a marketing guru, increased the market's acceptance of margarine by wrapping it in foil to suggest it was high-quality. This case of marketing strategy shows that our expectations about a food product are, in a way, an element of flavour.

From Mindlessness to Recognition to Savouring

Tasting (or flavour recognition) and savouring are related but not the same. Savouring begins with tasting. Tasting is sensing. Savouring is enjoying what you are sensing.

Our taste buds will recognise the four different tastes: sweetness, bitterness, sourness and saltiness. The enjoyment that you get from a certain food has a certain genetic component (we all have a different number of taste buds) but is also determined by your personal preferences, your level of hunger and the quality of the attention you pay to the act of eating.

How can you use your sense of taste to find a way of eating that pleases your taste buds and supports your body's health?

Try this:

Make time to choose a food that you really like, perhaps your favorite food, such as a piece of chocolate, some ice cream or a slice of pizza. Cut the food into small pieces.

For example, if you are using chocolate, cut it into four squares of about one inch each. Now take a few deep relaxing breaths, trying to centre yourself and become fully present in the moment. Begin to look at your first piece. Place it on your hand and experience temperature of the food you are eating. Is it hot, cold or room temperature?

Gently move the piece close to your nose and breathe in its aroma. Does the smell remind you of anything? Does it trigger an emotional reaction?

Become fully present for the experience of eating and the pleasure that it can bring. Place the piece of food in your mouth and begin to chew slowly. Explore the texture of the food: is it crispy, watery, chewy, creamy or dry? Then, very consciously, take one or two bites of it and notice what happens. Experience any waves of taste that emanate as you continue chewing. Let all of your attention be on the complete range of sensations available in each bite and feel the joy.

How satisfied are you after the first piece? Now take a second piece and repeat the sequence, with openness and curiosity. First look at the food, and then pay attention to the aroma. Do you notice any difference to the first piece? Begin to chew the food, paying special attention to the enjoyment you are getting from this tiny morsel. Decide to swallow, and rest while you wait to discover the aftertaste.

Take a third piece and lead yourself through the practice. What are your reactions? What is your mind telling you? Do you like it or dislike it? Any aversion or wanting more? Just acknowledge these thoughts and feelings and get gently back to the bare sensations of taste and texture in the mouth, and how these may change moment by moment. Once you have swallowed the third piece, take a few moments to decide if you would like a fourth. How are you making this choice? Is your mind or your body asking you to stop? How satisfied are you with the food you've had so far?

Whether you decided to eat the first piece of food or not, spend a few seconds to appreciate how this food came to be, the people involved in the process, and be thankful for any insight that your mind or body gave you.

***

This practice you just experimented with focuses specifically on taste and how the perception of taste changes as we eat. What have you noticed during the practice?

Did the food taste different as you kept eating? Were you chasing the flavour? Test your taste buds with different types of food, at different times of the day, and with an empty or full stomach, and see what surprises may be in store.

Smell

When it comes to eating, smell is an important sense. Aside from its role in appetite regulation, it more importantly tells us about what is edible and what is not, and thus serves as a survival guide.

As a trigger for eating, smell acts as a gateway drug in the sense that it introduces, molecule by molecule, our nose (and then our mind) to the intoxicating promise of food. Calling smell a "drug" is no exaggeration. After all, smell is chemistry: when we smell a given food, however far away from it our nose may be, we are, in fact, coming into direct contact with miniscule amounts of that food's particles that have randomly roamed into our nasal passages. So, if I smell chocolate, it means that while there may be no chocolate in sight, let alone in my mouth, there's already chocolate in my nose and on my mind. And, unless steered by a conscious mind, the mouth will blindly follow the nose to the source of the smell.

Movements of eating

Eating is a complex motor behaviour that consists of the coordination of arms, hands, neck and mouth. The kinesthetic awareness of eating involves monitoring your eating posture, your eating movements, the use of utensils and the specific kinesthetic signature of the given foodstuff. Becoming more aware of the movements of eating can help you learn to slow down and be more mindful of the eating experience.

Eating posture

Some eat sitting at the dining table, some eat on their recliner and some eat on the floor. Some eat standing at a bus stop, some at the kitchen countertop reading through the classifieds. Some eat lying down with a book. Explore posture for opportunities for mindfulness.

Eating movements

Eating movements are probably some of the best-practiced motor behaviours that we have in our repertoire. After all, we have been practicing them since birth. Eating involves perfectly choreographed hand-to-mouth coordination of multiple muscle groups working in flawless unison. In fact, eating movements are so basic that we do them without thinking.

The hypnosis of utensils

Utensils are part of the hypnotic ritual of eating. They cue our hands (and minds) to a certain complex of motor behaviours. As such, a utensil is an ignition key to the mindlessness of eating.

Kinesthetic signature

Each food has its own kinesthetic signature, or profile of eating movements. Eating a strawberry is different from eating a steak – if you're mindful, that is.

Write a step-by-step guide for eating popcorn. Pop some corn and document your experience. Be precise – skip nothing and specify everything. Make recommendations on how many popcorn clusters to clasp with your fingers to fit the serving into the average-sised mouth without dropping any of the pieces and give advice on how to deal with the unpopped kernels. Next, have a friend eat a bag of popcorn per your instructions. Have a laugh. Try this out with different foods. Why? Taking time to narrate an eating experience allows you to become aware of the subtle behavioural eating sequences that have previously slipped your mind.

Each food has its own kinesthetic profile, so how can we optimise it? Take spaghetti, for example. You can twirl it around on a fork or cut it up with a knife or lift it up and let your tongue pick up the hanging strands. What is the best way to do it? Analyse the kinesthetic signature involved in eating a particular foodstuff, and then try to improve the process by finding an alternative way of eating it. What criterion should you use for deciding when that optimisation has been achieved? That will depend on the food. If it is spaghetti, you can judge the tactic by how often a blob of spaghetti falls back onto the plate so the sauce stains your shirt. If you're spreading cream cheese on a cracker, you can tell by whether the cracker breaks from too much pressure applied to its surface. Granted, this is an exercise for eating geeks. But let's not forget that a defining characteristic of geekiness is presence of mind, albeit in matters of seeming irrelevance.

Sight

Food can be an aesthetic object. We describe food in terms of its visual presentation and sensual composition. We can also attribute aesthetic properties to food such as "elegant", "hearty" or "simple". For some of us, food is primarily the subject of aesthetic judgment about its appearance and only secondarily about nature and nutrition.

How can we use our eyes to mindfully guide us through our meal?

Here some simple questions that could show you the way: What does the food you are eating look like? Notice the colors of the food. Does it look appealing? Where does it come from? Is it a natural food you can recognise? A brief pause to assess your food can give you lots of information about it.

Also, if the way the food looks is important, try to satisfy your eyes with foods that are beautiful, colourful, and attractive that look like art miniatures. You can go further and consider matching your tableware to the specific dishes you are planning to eat. This might strike you as a bit strange, but strangeness is a precursor to mindfulness. Say you were to serve sushi in a kind of tableware you'd find in a sushi bar. The chances are you would, at least initially, pay attention to the aesthetics of the dish and, thus, also be more likely to pay attention to the food itself. Aside from trying to re-create the cultural ambience of the dish with culture-specific tableware, you could also think of tableware as a way to complement the appearance of the food. With this approach, you would be testing an artistic hypothesis and, therefore, remain more present during the meal. The bottom line is this: if you spend a moment deciding which plate will look good with the food, you will increase the chance that you will actually look at the food to see if the food does, indeed, look good with the plate you chose. And looking at the food is the beginning of paying attention to the process of eating it.

Bringing everything together: eat an apple using all your senses.

In a study by Julie Flood-Obbagy and Barbara Rolls, subjects were given a whole apple before a meal. People who ate an entire apple prior to lunch consumed fifteen percent less than those who had nothing at all before the meal. In part, the apple's fibre helps you to feel fuller and more satisfied.

Another hypothesis is that eating a pre-meal apple can shift you into a more mindful mindset. Consider what it's like to eat an apple or any other piece of fruit. Think about holding this piece of fruit in your hand. It's tangible, something you can put your hands around and actually feel. An apple stimulates all of your senses with its sweetness and loud crunch. Eating an apple takes time, effort and attention, it is a process that can move you from mindlessly consuming food to mindfully eating with awareness.

Try this mindful eating activity with an apple. For one week, eat an apple in this way every day. You can follow these steps:

1. At the supermarket, begin by mindfully choosing a type of apple that's pleasing to you, such as Gala (pinkish stripes on yellow skin, very sweet), Granny Smith (green and sour), Golden Delicious (golden, yellow, sweet), Mcintosh (blend of red and green, sweet with a tinge of sourness), or Red Delicious (red with a very sweet taste).

2. Place the apples in a fruit bowl or put one in your purse, backpack or briefcase. Be sure to have one in a handy and convenient place.

3. Take one apple out prior to eating a meal.

4. Hold the apple in your hand. Notice the colour and shape.

5. Feel the weight pulling your hand down.

6. Listen to the crunch as you chew.

7. Notice the texture. Draw your awareness to the juice and how the texture changes as you chew.

8. Inhale the sweet smell.

9. Continue with the next bite. Notice how it tastes.

10. After you eat the apple, take a few moments to appreciate how this food came to be, the soil, water

and sunshine that helped it grow, and how it came to you today.

11. Take a few relaxing breaths, and gently move on to the rest of your day, trying to keep this awareness with you.

Reflection:

How can you use your senses to overcome eating or to develop a joyful relationship with food? Write this down as you experiment eating with all your senses during this week.

Chapter 4: Reconnect with Your Physical Hunger and Satiety Cues

"What is always speaking silently is the body." - N. Brown

Mindful eating is getting popular and its ability to help people improve both their relationships with food and to support their weight management programmes is well-documented. We all have a certain innate tendency to eat as much as we can, as fast as we can, and store it so that we could survive a famine. Though it may become tiresome to say, our bodies want us to store fat so that it has reserves to access in case of ill-health or extreme circumstances. However, a combination of inactivity, lack of hard physical labor and a readily available food supply has caused us to never have to miss a meal, to be able to consume as many calories as needed and to enjoy ourselves far more than our bodies ever expected. The normal body signals are therefore overridden. The calorie density is affecting our basic consumptive quality and, as the quality of food has generally decreased, we are paying for it physically.

When we overeat, we override our body's want to stop with our mind's want for more taste, more action, more of everything. "Okay, I really shouldn't, but.,." Does this expression sound familiar? What we think is interesting in this expression is that it shows that you already know that what you are eating is not helping you get the type of relationship with food you want, and might even be damaging your health. In fact, the brain is the great equilibrator; it worries about us, and wants us to stay healthy, because if we die, it goes with us. It has one goal – survival.

Well, this works as a double-edged sword; on one hand, your brain wants you to eat as much as you can, but on the other, if you are eating junk food, your brain will eventually push you to eat healthier to make your body feel better. All of this is your brain running on auto-pilot, running on the basic principles of feast and famine, of association and generalisation.

This is all to say that when you begin to eat consciously, you will also find yourself more willing to try foods you once rejected, or foods you never considered. You will find yourself more willing to turn away from junk food, able to walk away from the unhelpful things with more ease or only mildly indulge yourself in the things that you once gorged on.

Mindful eating begins as a simple and easy to understand process. You eat whatever your body wants and then you stop when your body is satiated (satisfied, but not fully energised) or, if you are trying to just maintain weight, you stop when you are full.

Listening to the feedback of the body signals is helpful to connect you with your bodily wants. It also connects you with your actual hunger and fullness, so that you become skillful in knowing when to start and stop eating.

What are your bodily wants? As mentioned before, your body is pretty good in knowing that if you have just had too much chocolate, you really should not eat any more. In fact, you will probably tenuously eat something healthy that just begins to look good to you because it is not chocolate, or anything else that you can associate with overindulgence, and because of this, it will probably be healthier. Your body knows what it needs to survive, what it really wants and what is good for it.

It is curious how often we worry about what our body looks like, but from a physical point of view, we are not in touch with it at all. We ignore our bodies so much that we are even able to go through analgesic states. Have you ever hurt yourself and not noticed that you are hurt until you go somewhere and start to feel sore? We are not listening to what our bodies are telling us, and this includes all the messages that teach us how to self-regulate around food. For example, our actual hunger is routinely ignored as we are running our lives on a schedule. Some diets tell us to eat five or six or more meals a day whether we are hungry or not, others tell us to eat a big breakfast, a moderate lunch, and a small supper and stop.

So what is actual hunger?

Your actual hunger is your appetite. It is not a stasis thing, and it is not something that is programmed for "this much at this time" and "this much at this time". No, your appetite fluctuates because you fluctuate, and when you are in tune with your actual hunger, you might find out just how little you really need to eat to be satisfied and feel good. Of course, food choices can help you to feel fuller faster as well, such as protein and vegetables – protein for its thermic quality and natural appetite suppressants, and vegetables for their low calorie nutrient density that fills the stretch and density receptors in the stomach at a rate that makes it harder for you to overeat. However, as long as you are listening to your body, and are focused on your actual hunger, you are going to see yourself naturally eating less or more, but most importantly, you will be aligned with your needs.

It can be difficult to identify your actual hunger in the beginning as there are many factors than can interfere with our perception of hunger. Emotions, such as pain or anxiety can mimic the physical signals of hunger. Or if you are suffering from pain, you can either lose your appetite or you can try and use food as a suppressor of the pain. Then there's thirst. Your thirst can be a huge source to your hunger, in such a way that you might not even realise that you are thirsty and you might mistake it for hunger. You could keep eating and not understanding why you cannot feel full. That is because perhaps you were not hungry, you were thirsty, and you were giving the body the incorrect fuel.

***

Mindful practice – Reconnect with your Actual Hunger

Get comfortable in your chair, sitting with a straight but relaxed posture. Acknowledge your breath as it moves in and out your body. Close your eyes if it is comfortable. Now, take a few deep breaths and imagine that you are seated at the table with a meal in front of you.

Acknowledge any tension or thoughts about the food you are about to eat. Now check in with your stomach – how hungry are you on a scale of 1 to 10? From 1 not being hungry at all, to 10 being as hungry as possible. What are physical indicators of the actual hunger in your body?

Now, taking a few more deep breaths and thanking the body for any communication and insight that has happened, gently open your eyes when you are ready.

It might be difficult at first to reconnect with the physical signals of the hunger in your body. What did you discover? It could be helpful to experiment at different times of the day and check you hunger levels during meals.

***

Accepting hunger

Sometimes, hunger is a scary feeling. It is difficult to accept being a little uncomfortable as you wait for your next meal and endure not being as full as you want. Mindfulness is the practice of accepting this feeling.

Notice that this approach is different from liking the emotion. It is about learning to tell yourself "It is okay that I am a little uncomfortable". When you think "Two more hours until lunch, how will I possibly make it that long?" you could have a snack, or you could observe and honour your hunger as a message sent from the body. It means it is working properly and it is in need of energy.

***

Observe your fullness

Eating is a fascinating process. When on a diet, we don't eat when we are hungry, and when are off the diet, we eat when we are not hungry. The reasons we stop eating are no exception to this eating peculiarity. Here are just a few:

- You ran out of the food you like, so you stop eating. If you had the food you like, you would eat some more.

CINZIA PEZZOLESI, IVANA PLACKO

- You ran out of time. Back home after a long day at work, you stand in the kitchen grazing and browsing the mail. You feel guilty about putting your spouse or kids on hold as you promise that you will be up in five minutes to say good night. You have run out time, not out of food.

- Your plate is finally clean.

- You got your money's worth. Unsure if you got your money's worth, you make a few more trips to the buffet table.

When you are hungry, the following three sensations happen after you begin eating. First, the sensation of hunger goes away. This is a moment of hunger relief. This happens almost too fast for you to have time to enjoy your meal. If you stop eating at this point, then you no longer feel the painful emptiness of hunger, but you do not yet feel full. If you keep on eating, you will next experience a moment of pleasant fullness as the food distends the lining of your stomach, but not so much as to cause pain. If you keep on eating, you will eventually experience a moment of unpleasant fullness as the stomach distends to a painful degree.

Fullness (also known as satiety) fills the stomach, whereas satisfaction pleases the senses. In the search for quality of life, we often confuse satiety with satisfaction.

Often, it is only when we satisfy our sensory appetite that we feel we have finally had enough. The tradition of a dessert at the end of a meal is a perfect example of how we disregard the fullness of the tummy just to experience something yummy in the mouth. Jan Chozen Bays, a pediatrician and Zen teacher practicing in Oregon, expands on this topic and describes seven kinds of hunger including eye hunger, mouth hunger and nose hunger. She explains how we need to recognise what specific hunger is calling us and how to satisfy it without overloading our stomachs. So for example, if we are looking to satisfy our eye hunger, we need to have some beautiful or colourful food, or if it is the nose that needs satisfaction, we need to pay special attention to the aroma of what we are eating.

Sometimes, unhelpful self-talk can take us away from recognising being full. Here is what Rachel and Kathy, two of our clients, used to say:

- Rachel "I wish I could eat just the right amount. Instead, I eat large amounts and never feel really satisfied. I wish small bits of food filled me up, but they don't. I tell myself I'll stop when I'm full, but I never really get to "full" until it's too late and I feel sick to my stomach."

- Kathy "I hardly ever feel full. No matter how much I eat, even large portions, It doesn't seem to fill that space".

Such thoughts can interfere with our body signals and become a trigger for overeating. Similar to the difficulty of accepting hunger, we might desire a particular sensation and not feel "OK" until we have it. When you don't get what we want, you can feel uncomfortable and unsettled. Not feeling exactly as full as we want is a difficult sensation to tolerate and feels unfair.

Unfortunately, just because you intensely want and strive to feel full doesn't automatically mean that this desire is healthy and mindful. Perhaps you are striving to have a particular feeling, like happiness, pleasure or contentment, rather than to quiet a rumbling stomach.

If this is the case for you, your perception of fullness is probably a little off target. Years of yo-yo dieting and being served vast portion sizes at restaurants can disturb your perception of fullness. Reassure yourself that you can relearn these cues by bringing mindful awareness to the physical signals of fullness in your stomach.

***

Mindful practice – Reconnect with your Fullness

Get comfortable in your chair, sitting with a straight but relaxed posture. Acknowledge your breath as it moves in and out your body. Close your eyes if it's comfortable. Now, take a few deep breaths and imagine that you are seated at the table after having had a meal. Now check in with your stomach. How full are you right now on a scale of 1 to 10? From 1 not being full at all to 10 being as full as possible. What are the physical indicators of the fullness in your body?

Now, taking a few more deep breaths, and thanking the body for any communication and insight that might have happened, gently open your eyes when you are ready.

The sensation of being full might be experienced in different ways by different people. What did you discover in this practice? It could be helpful to check on your fullness at different times: before/half-way/just after your meal and 15 minutes later.

***

Conclusion

Recognising the physical signals of the body will help us distinghish between actual bodily needs and emotional and physiological needs. As you begin your journey to a more conscious, present and focused life, you will find it easier to differentiate between a perceived comfort in food and an actual want for it. You will be amazed at how often you will ask yourself "do I really want this?" and your body will respond, "no!" You will look at the food sitting there, maybe a pizza, maybe pasta, maybe chips and dip, or cake, or brownies, or another guilty pleasure out of the mass of possible guilty pleasures, and out comes a rationalisation, or excuse, saying, "I don't really want it... but... I could go for a little, just a little... I shouldn't... I don't even want it... but it looks real good." But when you stop and ask yourself "Do I really want this?" you get the answer "No". You'll be able to walk away and stop your brain from getting trapped in rationalisation and excuses. You will also be amazed, I have no doubt, at how often your body goes, "have some, get it, I want it", and that is 100% fine too.

Chapter 5: Making Mindful Food Choices

"When you feed yourself, you are feeding your life. Make wise choices so that you can grow into the person you were meant to be." - C. Wasserman

Mindful eating can help us make decisions more consciously. This ability derives from the fact that mindfulness breaks down the automaticity in our actions and allows us to tune in better to the feedback of our mind and body.

A recent research found that mindful attention "keeps strong temptations from developing in the first place." (Papies et al., 2014). In this study, the research team took 114 university undergraduates who were about to walk into the campus cafeteria. One third of them took a 12 minute course in mindfulness. Before they sat down to eat, two groups viewed images of healthy and unhealthy foods, but in one group, researchers told the students to "simply observe all their responses" and notice "how they arise, linger for a while and then dissipate, as passing mental states." A third group didn't see any photos, but were asked to scale their hunger. The group that took the mindfulness course consumed the same amount of calories, but made more healthy food choices (i.e. salads over chips). The findings demonstrated that mindful attention leads to healthier choice patterns among all participants, regardless of their dieting goals.

To develop your "mindful choice skill" you can start by bringing awareness to routine activities such as going into a coffee shop and choosing what to buy. You can than begin to look at the wide range of foods on offer: chocolates, biscuits, salads, sandwiches and more.

When you get asked "What would you like today?" make a mental note of what would be your first answer, a large coffee and chocolate cake, for example. However, as you are also beginning to practise mindful choices and bring awareness to the less conscious mechanisms that drive our eating behaviours, you can explore the variety of options that you have without having to rush into a decision. For example, you could decide to start with a drink and just order the coffee, and if after that you are still feeling hungry, you could order some food. Or you can bring attention to what is attracting you in that particular moment – is it something sweet, savoury or crunchy? What is the colour of the packaging? Can you spot an opportunity to nourish your body and your mind during your coffee break?

Mentally note if the enhanced awareness of your choices produces any change in your behaviour. If it is comfortable, you can experiment in your favourite place for 1 week. Please also note that eating mindfully does not mean that you have to make sensible decisions all the time and can't be a bit naughty in your choices. Mindfulness is about making conscious decisions, and sometimes those decisions include treating yourself to some guilt-free pleasures. In fact, mindfulness can help to heighten the pleasure if you are able to focus fully on your chosen treat.

Social occasions

One of the most difficult challenges for people who are struggling with food can be attending social occasions. It is particularly hard if this is an event where sharing food is charged with meaning, such as celebrating an event, gathering the whole family together, or being on holiday. It can feel quite uncomfortable to refuse food while everyone else seems to be enjoying themselves. Cravings may be easily triggered even if you have been practising mindful eating rigorously so far. It is therefore important to be able to activate our mindful choice muscle and avoid overeating without upsetting our hosts or looking awkward, or causing unnecessary suffering.

Here a list of things that you can experiment on to make the situation less of a challenge, such as:

- Arriving late at the buffet. It will be at the beginning of the event when people tend to pick the most appealing food. This is when the most serious eating takes place. It is best to visit the buffet when there is less tempting food left.

- Practising saying no to food. This might sound like an unnecessary preparation, but it really can make a difference. There will always be people who seem to take it as a personal insult if everyone else is not having the food they have made – this will often be somebody that is close to the family or friends. They can be persistent, and it can take a bit of practice to be able to refuse a dish gracefully. It is best to be prepared for them, and role playing can be good for this. By practising saying no, it will be easier to do this at the actual event. What are the phrases that you could use?

- Having a reason for not eating everything you get offered. You may not want to tell everyone your life story. It can therefore be helpful if you have a reason for not overeating. You do not have to lie, but there is also no obligation that you divulge personal information. Such questioning can be put to rest with a simple, "I do not eat this type of food" or "I don't eat after a certain time."

- Bringing along some memory aids. If you have a smart phone, you will be able to look at an inspiring quote or listen to a short mindful eating meditation if you are feeling vulnerable during the party.

- Sitting close to other people who you know are healthy eaters. It can be inspiring to see these people have a good time without the need to overeat.

- Practising pausing. If you know you are tempted to go down the overeating path, you can pause and turn your attention to these impulsive thoughts. This mindfulness allows you to dissect and recognise your feelings before they grow into an action plan to track down candy or comfort food.

The art of being flexible

What happens if, despite every effort you have made, you feel that you have already had a lot to eat and have ruined your plans anyway, so are tempted to continue indulging?. One of our participants once shared this story:

I was shopping in a popular book shop, when a woman offered me a free sample. It was a chocolate-chip mocha shake. The tiny cup was expertly finished with a swirl of whipped cream and a little red straw. I rolled my eyes and said, "Well, there goes the diet for today." That's all it took to get me off track.

—Michelle

There's a Zen saying that goes something like this: "The stiffest tree cracks the easiest, while the willow survives by bending with the wind." Just like the stiff tree, you can easily crack when your thoughts are too rigid. The thought "I have ruined it anyway" is a typical example of all-or-nothing thinking that represents some cognitive rigidity. Examples in other areas include when you think you are either perfect or a failure, fantastic or a loser. Rarely are you truly one way or the other.

Eating habits are a prime opportunity to develop an all-or-nothing mind-set. Let's go back to Michelle. She displayed rigid thinking in the book shop. Instead of bending a little and having a sip of the mocha drink, she allowed an all-or-nothing mind-set to take over. Thinking that she had ruined it anyway led her to abandon her efforts to eat well for the rest of the day.

By contrast, the mindful mind-set is characterised by openness and flexibility, responding to rigid thoughts like "There goes my diet for today" with an open mind. Mindfulness looks for what is called "the middle way", or the place between eating the whole thing or nothing. For example, you can assert "It's not completely ruined". The best way to stop yourself giving up when you have taken a misstep is to practise drawing your awareness to the middle way, or the grey areas, and being flexible in your thinking. For Michelle, this would mean telling herself that a sip of mocha is not a total failure.

Consider all-or-nothing thinking from this perspective. Say you drop a tiny spot of grape juice on your favourite white jumper. If you take care of the mishap that very moment, you can salvage the sweater. If you think "Well, it's ruined anyway", you are less likely to get the stain out before it sets. But is the jumper really ruined? It is unlikely that you would pour the rest of the glass of juice on it.

With food, we have many choices to make every day: what to eat, how, when and many more. The good news it that if we make a bad choice in one moment, we have many more chances to get things right. So, if you start binging on food, you can stop that binge at any time by making a different choice. You can look at the act of taking the food out of a container and stop there. You can look at taking the food out of the fridge and slam the door. Or you can have a first bite of something, and then leave the rest. Awareness of choices is the pillar of mindful eating and gives us flexibility and freedom.

Try this: rubber-band thinking

Train your mind to quickly identify the first hint of all-or-nothing thinking. When it happens, mentally dust yourself off and take a deep breath. Choose to respond mindfully to rigid thoughts by using "rubber-band thinking." Rubber-band thinking is flexible, and can stretch out beyond the limited categories of "always", "never", and "all or nothing".

Decide to change one aspect of your eating using rubber-band thinking for this week. For example, if you always eat your food standing and decide to change that habit, for the next few days see if you can reduce the instances to 4 times a week. Work and reevaluate your goals as you progress.

Choose not to graze

Grazing and picking at food can be difficult to stop. Maybe nibbling you're on this or that, or sitting in front of the TV mindlessly popping pretzels into your mouth at a party. To stop grazing you could try this practice:

MINDFULLY MOVE

Mindfully move.

1. Notice it. Simply observe in a non-judgmental way. Ask yourself "Why am I picking at food?"

2. Gauge your level of awareness on a scale from 1 to 10, where 1 means being zoned out, mindlessly munching, and 10 means being fully present, tasting each grain of salt.

3. Zoom in on the sensations and movements of your hands. This will help to pull you out of the unconscious movement of popping food into your mouth or picking at food. Look closely at the colour of the skin on your hands. Rub your fingertips together to feel the sensations. Notice their temperature. Focus on where your hands are placed. Describe how they feel on the table or your lap.

4. If you need imagery, clasp your hands together. Imagine holding a heavy paperweight in both hands. Visualise the weight firmly pulling your hands down into your lap. Imagine straining against the weight to pull your hands up when you have the urge to take a little nibble. Remember that grazing on food is a

habit and evidence that you have lapsed into autopilot behaviour.

5. Be curious of your reaction to this practice.

Chapter 6: Eat and Live with Awareness

"When you touch one thing with deep awareness, you touch everything." - Lao Tzu

Mindful eating grows out of a process of appreciation of food, the savouring of it, the true and full enjoyment of what you are eating. When you're doing mindful eating right, a piece of fruit becomes much more than a juicy sweet snack, it becomes a texture, a feel, multiple tastes filling your mouth as different regions of taste buds are touched and lit up, the feel of grains on the tongue, the move of the jaw causing a feeling of relaxation with each mastication. We allow ourselves to indulge, but so rarely do we enjoy, allowing something to melt away memorably in our mouths, remembering what each bite and taste was like. Often, the moment we eat something, we start on something else, and then move on to something else, then move back to the first thing we ate, with a dim memory, and a tainted taste.

There's a reason so many people add food into their sex lives. Food is not just an erotic substance, it's an intimate one, and since mindfulness is the process of self-intimacy, mindful eating is the natural second step, the process of intimately connecting ourselves to our reality by appreciating and connecting with the food we are eating. We have lost the intimacy in our own lives, our own connection with ourselves as we get caught up in the day to day frantic routine.

When you begin to appreciate something, even the slightest pleasure of a momentary break to slip a slice of orange between your lips, the cool citrus leaving a lingering tingle around your mouth, just for a second, as you work that piece of orange to your back teeth and bite down, filling your whole mouth with juice, a flood of sweet and sour, of citric goodness that touches all the different zones of your brain, you will begin to really enjoy your food. The texture of the fruit, the soft, moist skin between your teeth, grazing gently against your tongue as you work your teeth, more and more juice, less with each consecutive act of mastication, until the skin and pulp becomes a nice tasty mush that you are able to run over your tongue and move to the back of your throat and swallow down with a single gulp. You get to truly feel a connection with yourself that you probably rarely felt before, and with that realisation, you can take comfort that you can elicit that with every bite of orange, and look down, and see you still have an entire orange to go. (You could do this with any food).

It is appreciation, first and foremost, and mindful eating is appreciating the food that you are eating, enjoying it and savouring it. There are just so many qualities that you can appreciate that you probably have never even thought of, never noticed, never fully enjoyed. Mindful eating begins when your relationship is no longer about filling yourself but fully enjoying yourself in a way that keeps your body feeling good, which means you do not overeat and you don't under-eat to the point that you are starving.

Awareness it the way forward to connect with your food. Below is a check list for you to become more aware.

Eating awareness checklist

If you don't have time for anything else, just pay attention to these factors:

- Are you sitting while eating?
- Are you focusing only on your food rather than multitasking?
- Are you paying attention to habitual behaviours like picking at and grazing on food?
- Are you "popping" food into your mouth or eating slowly, one bite at a time?
- Are you truly tasting the food? Are you noticing the texture, flavour, temperature?
- Are you staying with this bite, thinking only about this one until you finish it completely?

- Are you gauging your level of hunger—really hungry, moderately hungry, very hungry—and eating accordingly?

- Are you gauging your fullness while eating? With each bite, ask yourself "How full am I?"

Meal Script – creating awareness from your first bite to the meal script

Eating as an activity, both at the level of a meal and the level of a bite, is acted out mindlessly in accordance with an over-rehearsed script with the often unhappy ending of overeating. I invite you to examine this conceptual plot and begin rewriting it.

At the level of a bite, eating may involve the following seven steps. Once you've decided to eat and what to eat, you next make (1) a decision about what specific part of the dish to eat first. This typically happens without much consciousness. Next is (2) the act of physically manipulating the morsel of food (with or without the utensils). In the case of finger food, you'd go from step 1 to step 3 which is the act of placing the food in your mouth. This may or may not be followed by 4, the act of consciously tasting and savouring the food. Following and/or in parallel with tasting, you'd proceed to (5) chew the food (which may or may not be conscious). After the chewing, you'd (6) swallow the food, and maybe (7) pause (with or without putting the utensils and/or food down) before the next bite. As you see, each bite is a complex series of steps of a behavioural autopilot that, on one hand, automates the process of eating and, on the other hand, begets the mindlessness of eating.

It is true that to break down each bite into separate steps is a bit pedantic. But how are we to breathe awareness into a meal without becoming aware of a single bite? With this advice in mind, to rewrite the bite script, to include yourself as a conscious protagonist in this play of life, practise infusing mindfulness into these otherwise mindlessly interlocked seven steps of taking a bite. And you can accomplish this with nothing more than just eating. You've heard this before: when you eat, just eat. To just eat, and not let your mind wander is a lot. But why should you just eat and not read a newspaper or watch TV? After all, it's just eating. But it's not just eating! Mindful eating is a commitment to being present; it's eating in real time. As such, mindful eating teaches one about the essence of time: time isn't measured in minutes; time is moments, moments of awareness. When unattended, these fleeting moments of our lives are lost from conscious experience, never to be recovered. Form a habit of starting your meal with just one bite. Mentally count from one to seven as you hold your consciousness, from deciding to take a bite, to identifying what to bite, to physically manipulating the food, to bringing it to your mouth, to the steps of tasting and chewing, to swallowing, and finally, to pausing. Pause to appreciate this moment of eating as a noteworthy moment of being alive.

Rewriting the script at a meal level

At the level of a meal, most eating episodes are staged to follow the three-act structure of prelude (an appetizer in the way of a soup, a salad or some finger food), the main act (a main course) and the climax (a dessert). But these acts aren't really acts unless they are mindfully enacted. An act, after all, involves an actor. An act without an actor is a reaction. Add a dollop of mindfulness to your meal to help you change the course of your eating.

What would change about the overall experience of the meal if you had dessert first? Would you then skip the appetizer and not rush through the main course just to get to the dessert, and eat less as a result? To paraphrase Pink Floyd, why should we, after all, have to eat meat before we can have any pudding? Try eating dessert first a few times to see what, if any effect, this kind of re-sequencing might have on the state of your mind and the state of your body.

It is hard to bring awareness and a connection to food if we don't bring awareness to the rest of our lives. If we never find time to stop, how can we just focus on our eating?

As mentioned in the initial chapter, mindfulness meditation is closely linked to mindful eating. According to The Centre for Mindful Eating (TCME, 2014), mindful meditation can be a very valuable support for the practice of mindful eating. Meditation promotes many of the principles of mindful eating, including paying attention without judgment and being aware of thoughts, feelings and all the senses while eating.

Here are some practices to shape your awareness muscle:

Mindfulness of breathing

You can practice paying attention to your breathing for 10 minutes every day. If you have little time, just practise this meditation for 2 minutes before your meals.

This guided meditation on your breathing will help you learn to simply be and to look within yourself with mindfulness and equanimity. Allow yourself to switch from the usual mode of doing to a mode of non-doing. Of simply being. Sitting with an erect posture, either on a straight back chair or on a cushion. As you allow your body to become still, bring your attention to the fact that you are breathing. And become aware of the movement of your breath as it comes into your body and as it leaves your body. Not manipulating the breath in any way or trying to change it. Simply being aware of it and of the feelings associated with breathing. And observing the breath deep down in your belly. Feeling the abdomen as it expands gently on the in-breath, and as it falls back towards your spine on the out-breath. Being totally here in each moment with each breath. Not trying to do anything, not trying to get any place, simply being with your breath. Giving full care and attention to each in-breath and to each outbreath. As they follow one after the other in a never ending cycle and flow.

You will find that from time to time your mind will wander off into thoughts. When you notice that your attention is no longer here and no longer with your breathing, and without judging yourself, bring your attention back to your breathing and ride the waves of your breathing, fully conscious of the duration of each breath from moment to moment. Every time you find your mind wandering off your breathing, gently bringing it back to the present, back to the moment-to-moment observing of the flow of your breathing. Using your breath as an anchor to focus your attention, to bring you back to the present whenever you notice that your mind is becoming absorbed or reactive. Using your breath to help you tune into a state of relaxed awareness and stillness.

Now as you observe your breathing, you may find from time to time that you are becoming aware of sensations in your body. As you maintain awareness of your breathing, see if it is possible to expand the field of your awareness so that it includes a sense of your body as a whole as you sit here. Feeling your body, from head to toe, and becoming aware of all the sensations in your body. So that now you are observing not only the flow of breathing, but the sense of your body as a whole.

Being here with whatever feelings and sensations come up in any moment without judging them, without reacting to them, just being fully here, fully aware. Totally present with whatever your feelings are and with your breath and a sense of your body as a whole. And again whenever you notice that your mind wandering off, just bringing it back to your breathing and your body as you sit here not going anywhere, not doing anything just simply being, simply sitting. Moment to moment, being fully present, fully with yourself.

Reestablishing your awareness on the body as a whole and on the breath as it moves in and out of your body. Coming back to a sense of fullness of each in-breath, and the fullness of each outbreath. If you find yourself at any point drawn into a stream of thinking and you notice that you are no longer observing the breath, just using your breathing and the sense of your body to anchor you and stabilize you in the present.

Just being with your breathing from moment to moment, just sitting in stillness, looking for nothing and being present to all. Just as it is, just as it unfolds. Just being right here, right now. Complete. Human. Whole.

As the practice comes to an end, you might give yourself credit for having spent this time nourishing yourself in a deep way by dwelling in this state of non-doing, in this state of being. For having intentionally made time for yourself to simply be who you are. And as you move back into the world, allow the benefits of this practice to expand into every aspect of your life.

Reference: Mindfulness Meditation, CD Series 1, Jon Kabat-Zinn

Mindfulness of the body

Being aware and appreciating the body is key to developing a good connection with yourself and having a more integrated approach towards life. Experiment reconnecting with the body by doing the Body Scan practice:

1. Sit in a chair for the breath awareness or lie down, making yourself comfortable, lying on your back on a mat or rug on the floor or on your bed. Choose a place where you will be warm and undisturbed. Allow your eyes to close gently.

2. Take a few moments to get in touch with the movement of your breath and the sensations in the body. When you are ready, bring your awareness to the physical sensations in your body, especially to the sensations of touch or pressure, where your body makes contact with the chair or bed. On each out-breath, allow yourself to let go, to sink a little deeper into the chair or bed.

3. Remind yourself of the intention of this practice. Its aim is not to feel any different, relaxed, or calm; this may happen or it may not. Instead, the intention of the practice is, as best you can, to bring awareness to any sensations you detect, as you focus your attention on each part of the body in turn.

4. Now bring your awareness to the physical sensations in the lower abdomen, becoming aware of the changing patterns of sensations in the abdominal wall as you breathe in, and as you breathe out. Take a few minutes to feel the sensations as you breathe in and as you breathe out.

5. Having connected with the sensations in the abdomen, bring the focus or "spotlight" of your awareness down the left leg, into the left foot, and out to the toes of the left foot. Focus on each of the toes of the left foot in turn, bringing a gentle curiosity to investigate the quality of the sensations you find, perhaps noticing the sense of contact between the toes, a sense of tingling, warmth, or no particular sensation.

6. When you are ready, on an in-breath, feel or imagine the breath entering the lungs, and then passing down into the abdomen, into the left leg, the left foot, and out to the toes of the left foot. Then, on the outbreath, feel or imagine the breath coming all the way back up, out of the foot, into the leg, up through the abdomen, chest, and out through the nose. As best you can, continue this for a few breaths, breathing down into the toes, and back out from the toes. It may be difficult to get the hang of this just practice this "breathing into" as best you can, approaching it playfully.

7. Now, when you are ready, on an out-breath, let go of awareness of the toes, and bring your awareness to the sensations on the bottom of your left foot—bringing a gentle, investigative awareness to the sole of the foot, the instep, the heel (e.g., noticing the sensations where the heel makes contact with the mat or bed). Experiment with "breathing with" the sensations—being aware of the breath in the background, as, in the foreground, you explore the sensations of the lower foot.

8. Now allow the awareness to expand into the rest of the foot—to the ankle, the top of the foot, and right into the bones and joints. Then, taking a slightly deeper breath, directing it down into the whole of the left foot, and, as the breath lets go on the out-breath, let go of the left foot completely, allowing the focus of awareness to move into the lower left leg—the calf, shin, knee, and so on, in turn.

9. Continue to bring awareness, and a gentle curiosity, to the physical sensations in each part of the rest of the body in turn - to the upper left leg, the right toes,

right foot, right leg, pelvic area, back, abdomen, chest, fingers, hands, arms, shoulders, neck, head, and face. In each area, as best you can, bring the same detailed level of awareness and gentle curiosity to the bodily sensations present. As you leave each major area, "breathe in" to it on the in-breath, and let go of that region on the out-breath.

10. When you become aware of tension, or of other intense sensations in a particular part of the body, you can "breathe in" to them—using the in-breath gently to bring awareness right into the sensations, and, as best you can, have a sense of their letting go, or releasing, on the outbreath.

11. The mind will inevitably wander away from the breath and the body from time to time. That is entirely normal. It is what minds do. When you notice it, gently acknowledge it, noticing where the mind has gone off to, and then gently return your attention to the part of the body you intended to focus on.

12. After you have "scanned" the whole body in this way, spend a few minutes being aware of a sense of the body as a whole, and of the breath flowing freely in and out of the body.

13. If you find yourself falling asleep, you might find it helpful to prop your head up with a pillow, open your eyes, or do the practice sitting up rather than lying down.

14. You can adjust the time spent in this practice by using larger chunks of your body to become aware of or spending a shorter or longer time with each part.

Practise mindfulness of the body three times a week for one month.

Chapter 7: How to Take This Forward

"Move, and the way will open." - Zen proverb

Are you ready for the mindful eating journey?

"I want to lose weight so badly. After having two kids and going back to school for my nursing degree, I put on a few extra pounds. Every morning, when I get ready to go to work and scramble to get the kids dressed for school, I vow that today will be the day I start watching what I eat. But inevitably, by midmorning, a rumbling stomach and hectic pace at the ER leave me craving something sweet and gooey. I have the best intentions to lose weight but just can't seem to get the ball rolling. Thinking that I just can't get started keeps me at square one." —Linda

Like many people, Linda has the Scarlett O'Hara approach to mindful eating: I will think about that tomorrow. Who has not declared a plan to initiate change tomorrow, next week or after some upcoming event? We often say such things simply to soothe ourselves. Having a plan keeps your anxiety in check, even if you have no intention of carrying it out.

If you commonly say these things to yourself, pay attention to how and when you say them. Do you wink as you announce to your friends that you will start your diet tomorrow? Or do you reflexively say this to yourself the moment you pick up a high-calorie or greasy food? Maybe you make this statement on autopilot. You talk about tomorrow without genuine feeling or without even really thinking about what it means. Sometimes you really mean it; you tell yourself you will get started the next day, but, more often than not, this is a way of avoiding making any real changes.

Take a moment right now to do a self-check. Ask yourself: "If I started tomorrow, what would I expect of myself?" What pops into your mind? Does a long list of behavioural changes flash before your eyes? Maybe it includes things like cutting out sweets, eating only healthy snacks, stopping eating as a result of stress, and so on. Are your expectations too high or unobtainable? When your expectations are so far from where you stand right now, you set yourself up for frustration and failure. It is like asking someone who has only ever run a mile to run a marathon. Notice your emotional reaction to the Scarlett O'Hara mind-set versus the mindful one: "I must run a marathon tomorrow" versus "I will focus on taking one baby step at a time today". Which seems more doable and approachable? Take some time to reflect on your expectations and readiness to change.

Common obstacles in your journey

Lack of time

"Who has time to eat healthily or exercise? I barely have time to get dressed in the morning. If I don't make time, six months will go by and I'll be in exactly the same place I'm in now." —Victoria

As a mom, wife, full-time teacher and part-time musician, Victoria wears many hats. Whenever she thinks about eating better, her mind goes directly back to the same thought: "Who has the time?" Like many busy women, she can get ten different projects done in one day, but changing her eating habits rarely makes the top of her to-do list.

If the lack-of-time excuse sounds familiar to you, you are probably putting off eating healthier and more mindfully until a time when life will slow down. Remind yourself that you will probably never find a time that is quieter or less busy than today. As the Greek philosopher Heraclitus of Ephesus stated: "You can never step into the same river, for new waters are always flowing onto you."

The good news is that mindful eating doesn't take a lot of time. Why? Because you don't have to drastically change what you eat or drive miles out of the way to go to a special grocery store. Instead, do what you already do but with more awareness. This should take no additional time. For example, imagine that you make dinner for your family each night. You think you don't have time to cook anything different from your usual meals. Instead of altering the menu, first try bringing mindfulness to what you already eat. If you eat pizza, work on eating that pizza mindfully. Through this attentive awareness, you will naturally change the way you eat, and sometimes, what you eat, too. Pause for a second before eating your next snack or meal. Ask yourself: "How can I approach this meal more mindfully?"

Feeling stuck

"I've been stuck at the same weight for six weeks. I feel as if I have found a parking spot and refuse to give it up. I can't move. I've tried everything: attempting to snack less, eating more, increasing the amount of exercise I do, decreasing the amount of exercise I do, eating everything in sight, eating only salad… I don't know how to get past this." - Alexa

Sir Isaac Newton explained the concept of inertia, which is the natural resistance of an object to a change in motion. An object will stay at rest or in motion until an external force acts on it. For example, a ball will stay still until a force is applied to it. Once the ball gets going, it takes another force, perhaps applied by a person, to stop it. In many ways, the law of inertia also can apply to life and, particularly, to eating. You may feel like that ball. Inside, you feel stagnant and unable to move forward. Your mind keeps saying "I cannot change, because I am stuck."

The foot-in-the-door technique is a psychological approach that can help you get started and give you a little push. Traditionally, this technique involves getting a person to agree to a big favour by having that person agree to a smaller one first. For example, if you want someone to babysit for three hours, start by asking for fifteen minutes of babysitting time, which the person probably will agree to. Once the person is hooked by this request, it's easier to obtain a greater commitment. You can use the same technique to start the process of mindful eating. If you can't agree to the seemingly large request to eat mindfully today, make a much more modest request of yourself, something you know you can easily do. Choose a very small action. For example, if you are eating a bag of crisps, ask yourself to skip one bite. Turn your attention to how this small request feels. Is it overwhelming? Does it feel "OK"? If so, make a slightly bigger request. How about two bites? Turn your attention to how this feels physically and emotionally.

Rationalising

"I have all sorts of compelling reasons why I can't eat mindfully now: I've had the flu, I've been dealing with a crisis at work, my child got in trouble at school, I celebrated my thirtieth birthday. The list of ways I can rationalise mindless eating could go on and on. But the reality is that when I fudge a little bit here and there, I end up feeling horrible. It typically starts out in small ways, like nibbling on an extra bite or two. The more I indulge, the more excuses I find to justify mindless eating. - Jessica

Jessica's mind tried to explain why it was "OK" to eat mindlessly. Interestingly, many reasons for mindless eating sound perfectly rational. For example, you may argue that you don't want your food to go to waste, or justify eating another slice of pie by insisting that refusing to do so would offend your grandmother. Why do these justifications and rationalisations happen? When you act in ways that are contradictory to mindful eating, the mind has to come up with an explanation or justification. It creates a mental bridge to help explain the gap. Rationalising techniques include discounting, excusing, justifying, denying, and pretending that things are different to how they really are. Rationalising statements include things like "It's okay just this one time and these calories don't really count."

Respond mindfully to your rationalisations. Firstly, gently acknowledge your rationalisation. Next, identify the self-serving purpose of the rationalisation. Finish this sentence: "Rationalising mindless eating is serving the purpose of..." For example, you might think "Rationalising mindless eating is serving the purpose of reducing guilt" or "It may allow me to avoid making a decision by convincing me that I don't have a real choice." Try to be honest about your motivation. Instead of deeming your behaviour to be right or wrong, as you do when you justify things, just describe what you want to eat—or what you ate—and why. The less judgmental you are, the more honest you will be with yourself. For example, let's say your mind is trying to justify eating dessert. You think "It's OK. I have to eat it because my kids are insisting that I have dessert". A mindful approach would simply describe what happened, without judging whether it is right or wrong. You would tell yourself "The kids are insisting I have dessert." Listen to what your body tells you about this option as you merely describe your dilemma.

Issues around food sustainability

"I have school clothes to buy for my kids, a mortgage and too many other bills to pay. I can't afford to eat healthily. Healthy food costs so much. I don't know how I will ever turn this around, unless the government makes healthy food cheap for people like me, who are just getting by and paying their bills." – Jennie

Being short on cash is a very real deterrent for people like Jennie who are trying to change their eating habits. It is true that gym memberships cost money. Healthy food can be more expensive than fast-food. Such foods are cheaper, in part, due to state subsidies for most grain products used to make corn syrup for sweeteners, baked goods and other processed foods. Some parts of your financial worries are real barriers, but other times, they can be another example of 'detour thoughts'.

The other side of the coin is that being overweight is also financially draining. The cost of being overweight is high, taking money directly out of your pocket in several ways. Obesity significantly increases healthcare costs. This may be in the form of higher insurance rates, more doctor's appointments, medicine for weight-related illnesses, and missed work without pay. Often, the most tangible cost is often unrelated to your bank account. Extra weight drains self-esteem and can complicate your relationships and health. Jennie's weight, for example, was literally killing her. Her weight had slowly increased over the years to the point where she was taking medication for diabetes. Although her medication was expensive, the psychological cost was even more devastating. She was not able to kneel down on the floor to play with her children or walk a few blocks to the park. Jennie didn't take her kids swimming, because there was no way she would allow anyone to see her in a swimming costume. Life just was not as enjoyable as it could have been. "How did I let it get like this?" she wondered with regret. To her, the cost of healthy food and the price of being overweight were both high. Eating healthily saved her money in the long run. She bought less food overall and stopped wasting money on impulse buys.

When your mind says you do not have enough cash to change your eating habits, close your eyes and imagine that six months from now, nothing has changed. Notice what feelings and thoughts arise as you contemplate this scenario. Where do you feel discomfort - in your heart, your body, your self-esteem? Draw your attention to the emotional, physical and psychological costs of staying stuck exactly where you are in this very moment.

Sure, you could come up with an entire list of free or low-cost ways to tackle the problem: taking walks outdoors, using coupons, not ordering so much fast food, cooking, cutting out unnecessary junk food and so on. But perhaps it is not just about money. It is about valuing yourself and knowing how much you think you are worth.

Practice: Minding the Cost

Be more mindful of how much money you spend on food. For one week, each time you buy food, whether you eat out, purchase groceries or buy a snack at a convenience store, keep the receipt. After you eat, draw your attention to how each food purchase makes your body feel. Write about your experience on the back of the receipt. Tally up how much money you spend on healthy food and how much you spend on unhealthy options. Also, factor in how much medicine costs you, as well as any "diet" products you may use. Begin to think of each food purchase as a small investment in yourself, in your health and self-esteem. Respond to "I can't afford" it with "I can't afford not to eat healthily."

How can you facilitate the process of change?

Some self-care behaviours are not optional. Somehow, in our busy lives, we find time to shower, brush our teeth and do a number of other things that take time. It would be nice if we could think of healthy eating and exercise in this manner, as compulsory rather than optional. But the reality is that it is not that simple.

To facilitate the process of eating mindfully you could:

- **Link mindful eating behaviours to already established, routine behaviours.** For example, sometimes people take their medications after brushing their teeth. Perhaps you could mindfully pack a healthy snack for work before showering each evening or go shopping for healthy foods every week after religious services.

- **Make the task of eating healthily and mindfully as easy as possible so you don't have to exert too much effort.** You are more likely to eat what is convenient than what you like. You can use this principle to your advantage. Keep healthy food in an easy-to-reach location. Place a fruit bowl on your counter in your direct sight path.

- **Make grazing on and picking at food inconvenient and difficult.** Hide food in the back of your cupboard, in the freezer or on the top shelf. You will only invest time in retrieving them if you really want them. Changing the storage location of your snacks could be a simple but effective trick to reduce mindless eating.

- **Curb your motivation.** Is there anything that might keep your motivation to eat mindfully high? Perhaps you could turn your attention to the reasons why eating mindfully is important for you. Maybe you want to eat more mindfully to be a good role model for your kids, or perhaps you want your clothes to fit better. If so, the trick is to keep these reasons in the forefront of your mind. The motives can be easily pushed to the back of your mind or slip out of your awareness.

- **Keep your awareness in good shape** – establish a mindfulness meditation routine. It could be anything from one mindful breath a day to ten minutes a day, or even much longer if you feel comfortable with that.

- **Write a letter to yourself.** Reflect on your learning and develop a list of actions that could support you. Write a letter to yourself and store it in a special place. Review your letter every three months.

Dear (your name)

Well done for adventuring into the fascinating journey of mindful eating. During this process you have learnt that

practicing mindful eating has helped you

Please remember that you can support your mindful eating path by doing the following things

With love,

(your name)

Finally, this book is just the beginning of your journey. Seek out new information and find new resources. We found the resources below very helpful, but just take this list as a way to spark your interest.

Journal Articles

Albers, Susan. Eat, Drink and Be Mindful: How to End Your Struggle with Mindless Eating and Start Savoring Food with Intention and Joy. New Harbinger Publications, 2009.

Altman, Don. Meal by Meal: 365 Daily Meditations for Finding Balance Through Mindful Eating. New World Library, 2009.

Caldwell, Karen L., Michael J. Baime, and Ruth Q. Wolever. "Mindfulness based approaches toobesity and weight loss maintenance." Journal of Mental Health Counseling 34.3 (2012): 269.Full text: http://www.biomedsearch.com/article/Mindfulness-based-approaches-to-obesity/297915511.html

Godsey, Judi. "The role of mindfulness based interventions in the treatment of obesity and eating disorders: An integrative review." Complementary Therapies in Medicine (2013).

Jazaieri, Hooria, and Shauna L. Shapiro. "Managing Stress Mindfully." Contemplative Practices

Paolini, Brielle, et al. "Coping with brief periods of food restriction: mindfulness matters. Frontiers in aging neuroscience 4 (2012). Full text: http://www.ncbi.nlm.nih.gov/pmc/articles/

Timmerman, Gayle M., and Adama Brown. "The Effect of a Mindful Restaurant Eating Intervention on Weight Management in Women." Journal of nutrition education and behavior 44.1 (2012): 22-28. Full text: http://www.ncbi.nlm.nih.gov/pmc/articles/PMC3259454/

Books:

Bays, Jan Chozen. Mindful Eating. Shambhala Publications, 2009

Web-based resources

The Centre For Mindful Eating (TCME). TCME is an international not-for-profit forum for professionals across all disciplines interested in developing, deepening and understanding the value and importance of mindful eating. http://www.thecenterformindfuleating.org

Final Note

Thank you for taking the time to read this book. By doing so, you have taken a radical step towards living a healthier, more mindful life. We hope that you will continue on your path of finding joy and peace with food, remaining curious regarding your new lifestyle, and grateful for any personal developments that you should undergo along the way.

For additional resources and online courses, we invite you to visit our website:

www.TheArtOfMindfulEating.co.uk

ABOUT THE AUTHORS

 **Cinzia Pezzolesi** is a chartered Clinical Psychologist and Mindfulness Based Cognitive Therapist. She is the Clinical Director at The Mindfulness Project. She qualified as a mindfulness teacher at the University of Bangor (North Wales, UK), and trained as Mindful Eating trainer in Boston (USA). She is a board member of the Centre for Mindful Eating in the USA. She has a PhD in Human Factors in Health Care and obtained her Clinical Psychologist degree from the University of Urbino, in Italy where she is originally from. She currently lives in the UK, and over the years she has developed a strong research interest around wellbeing and mindfulness in various settings. Her areas of expertise include anxiety, depression, eating disorders and vocational rehabilitation.

**Ivana Placko** received a degree in Management Information System and an MBA from the Oral Roberts University in Tulsa, OK, USA. She works for Gallup, an American research-based, global performance-management consulting company. As an ex-professional athlete and successful business woman, she is very passionate about mindful eating and understanding how it can improve both physical and mental performance.

10420703R00080

Printed in Great Britain
by Amazon.co.uk, Ltd.,
Marston Gate.